Scary Creatures
of the
RAIN FOREST

Written by
Penny Clarke

FRANKLIN WATTS
An Imprint of Scholastic Inc.
NEW YORK • TORONTO • LONDON • AUCKLAND • SYDNEY
MEXICO CITY • NEW DELHI • HONG KONG
DANBURY, CONNECTICUT

Created and designed
by David Salariya

Author:

Penny Clarke is an author and editor specializing in nonfiction books for children. She has written books on natural history, rain forests, and volcanoes, as well as books on various periods in history. She used to live in central London, but thanks to modern technology she has now realized her dream of being able to live and work in the countryside.

Artists:
John Francis
Robert Morton
Carolyn Scrace
Nicholas Hewetson
Terry Riley
Mark Bergin
Shirley Willis
Lizzie Harper

Series Creator:

David Salariya was born in Dundee, Scotland. In 1989 he established The Salariya Book Company. He has illustrated a wide range of books and has created many new series for publishers in the U.K. and overseas. He lives in Brighton, England, with his wife, illustrator Shirley Willis, and their son.

Editor: Stephen Haynes

Editorial Assistants:
Rob Walker, Tanya Kant

Picture Research:
Mark Bergin, Carolyn Franklin

Photo Credits:

t=top, b=bottom

Tom Brakefield/Verve: 15b, 18, 22, 25
Cadmium: 8, 15t
John Foxx Images: 12
Mountain High Maps/© 1993 Digital
   Wisdom Inc.: 6–7
Photodisc: 4
PhotoSpin Inc.: 11

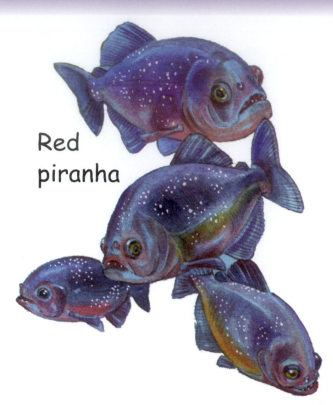

Red piranha

Created, designed, and produced by
The Salariya Book Company Ltd
Book House
25 Marlborough Place
Brighton BN1 1UB

A CIP catalog record for this title is available from the Library of Congress.

ISBN-13: 978-0-531-20544-0 (Lib. Bdg.)
      978-0-531-21010-9 (Pbk.)
ISBN-10: 0-531-20544-4 (Lib. Bdg.)
      0-531-21010-3 (Pbk.)

Published in the United States by Franklin Watts
An Imprint of Scholastic Inc.
557 Broadway
New York, NY 10012

Printed in China.

PAPER FROM

SUSTAINABLE FORESTS

Contents

Goliath beetle

What is a Rain Forest?

This book is about **tropical** rain forests. Forests grow all over the world, but different types of plants grow in different conditions and climates. Plants in tropical rain forests need at least 80 inches (200 cm) of rain that falls evenly throughout the year and an almost constant temperature of 79° Fahrenheit (26°C). Only tropical regions of the world have these conditions.

Tropical rain forests are richer in plants and animals than anywhere else on Earth. Most rain forest trees are very tall, growing to about 165 feet (50 m), but a few reach 200 feet (60 m). These huge trees provide different **habitats** for the thousands of **species** living in rain forests.

Emerald tree boa

Emerald tree boas kill by wrapping themselves around and choking their **prey**.

Emerald
tree boa

Heliconid
butterfly

Red-eyed tree frog

Topaz
hummingbird

Poison arrow
frog

Leaf-cutter ant

5

Where Are the Rain Forests?

You'll find tropical rain forests in South and Central America, Africa, and Southeast Asia. They grow only in tropical lowlands because those regions have the perfect climate for tropical rain forests.

Anacondas are snakes that crush their prey.

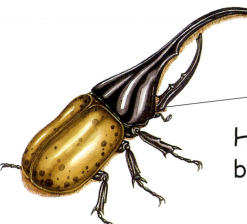

Anaconda

Hercules beetle

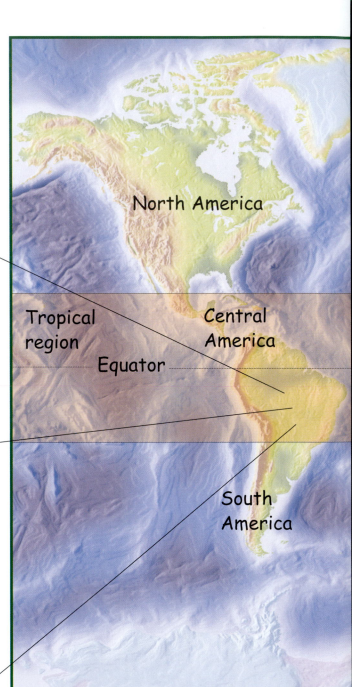

North America

Tropical region

Central America

Equator

South America

Common caiman

Caimans live in the rivers of the Amazon rain forest.

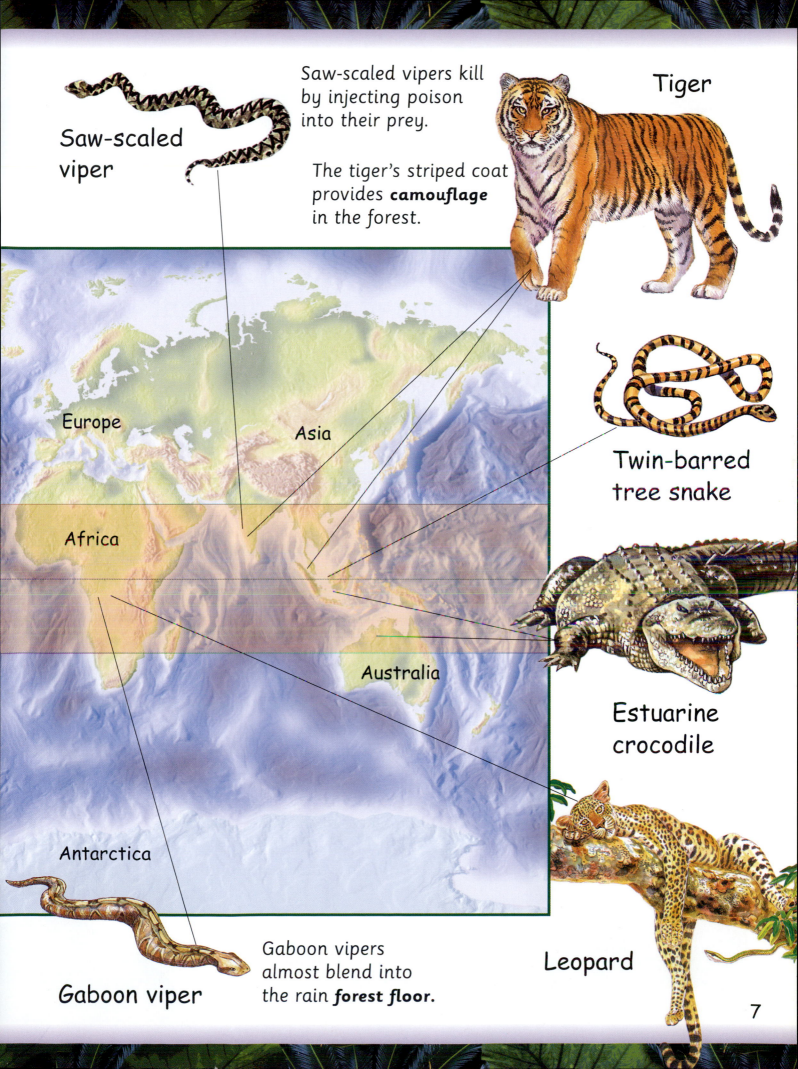

Saw-scaled viper

Saw-scaled vipers kill by injecting poison into their prey.

Tiger

The tiger's striped coat provides **camouflage** in the forest.

Europe

Asia

Africa

Australia

Antarctica

Twin-barred tree snake

Estuarine crocodile

Leopard

Gaboon viper

Gaboon vipers almost blend into the rain **forest floor.**

7

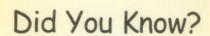

Did You Know?
In a rain forest more plants grow
on the trees than on the ground!

What Is Interdependence?

Every habitat is the home of many different species. Take away one species, and some others would not survive because each one depends on several others. This is called interdependence. Rain forest trees provide homes for hundreds of animals, but the trees depend on the animals, too.

Why do plants need animals?

Plants need insects to **pollinate** their flowers. They need birds and other animals to spread their seeds by eating their fruit.

Scientists estimate that every 2.5 acres (1 hectare) of tropical rain forest has about 750 species of trees, 1,500 other species of plants, and 42,000 species of insects—and that's not counting all the birds, reptiles, amphibians, and **mammals**!

Pitcher plant

Pitcher plants trap insects in their "pitchers."

8

Keel-billed toucan

Cotton topped tamarin

Red-faced uakari

Saw-billed hermit hummingbird

Woolly monkey

Pierid butterfly

Spider monkey

Red howler monkey

Jaguar

Tree porcupine

Squirrel monkey

Are Rain Forests Dark and Scary?

It depends where you are. Rain forest trees are so tall and have such thick, leafy tops that little light reaches the ground. So at ground level it is very dark, but in the treetops it is light.

Tarantulas look much more scary than they are. They feed on insects, young birds, lizards, and frogs.

Meeting a jaguar in the rain forest would be very scary!

Tarantula

What Lives in the Canopy?

Because the canopy is bright and sunny, more creatures live there than anywhere else in the rain forest. Brilliantly colored birds and butterflies dart about in the canopy, feeding on the bright flowers and fruit.

X-Ray Vision

Hold the next page up to the light to see some of the creatures that live in the rain forest canopy.

See what's inside

Birds' beaks tell you what they eat. Hummingbirds have long, thin beaks to reach nectar deep inside flowers. Macaws (right) crack open nuts with their small, tough beaks. Toucans (below) pick fruit with their long, curved beaks.

Toucan

Macaw

Toucans also grab eggs from other birds' nests with their big beaks.

The trees of the canopy are not the tallest in the forest. A few even taller ones soar above them. These are the "forest giants" of the emergent layer, so named because they emerge from the rest of the rain forest.

Harpy eagle

Macaw

Hummingbird

Morpho butterfly

13

Howler monkey

Squirrel monkey

Three-toed
sloth

Do Monkeys Live in the Rain Forest?

Yes! Wherever there are rain forests, there are monkeys. The calls of the howler monkey echo across the forest. Squirrel monkeys scamper through the canopy and into the emergent layer, where danger may hover as a harpy eagle flies overhead. But the greatest threat is loss of habitat as rain forests are felled.

Squirrel monkey

Squirrel monkeys live in the South American rain forest. They use their long tails to help them balance as they jump from tree to tree searching for food.

Orangutans live only in the rain forests of Southeast Asia. They can use their powerful arms to swing through the trees, but they usually walk along branches (and on the ground) on all fours or upright.

Female orangutan with baby